THE FACE *in the* NIGHT SKY

THE FACE
in the
NIGHT SKY

poetry to engage your soul

LANA LENSMAN

ISBN 979-8-9875062-0-2 (print)
ISBN 979-8-9875062-1-9 (e-book)

First Edition
Cover design by Holly Forrest

CONTENTS

NEW MOON 2

NEW MOON 3

Close your eyes. Point your finger and touch the mandala.

Open your eyes to see the poem that wants to engage with you.

Each poem offers an entry-point into the soul journey.

It will guide you inward, a slow spiral into the heart of creation.

Replicating nature's way, the energy of the mandala wants to

find center and then return, moving outward into life expression.

Blank Mind Perfection Containment Loneliness Alone Shadow True Origin Wisdom Seeker Silence One Heart Wisdom

Calm Waters Alignment Quiet Mind Early Morning The Gathering In the Stillness Unnamed Breath of Life Reclaimed

The Unsought Your Life Movie The Cage Self-Doubt The Stranger Listen Deeply Voices of Past Surface Layer

The Journey The New World The Path Ahead The Discovery Be Brave Soul Wisdom Travel Deep Present Instant Replay Trying Polarity The River

Road Trip Memories Full Moon's Light Spirit Wind Lift it Up The Sacred Well Meet Me The Promise Burning Desire Luxury Expectation

Soul Impression Inhale Deeply Interwoven Going To The Gap Love Match The 11 Expressway Separate Earth Serenity Daily Dance Immersed

Unknown Waters

INTRODUCTION

This poetry collection is meant to transport you beyond the mind into a profound dialogue with your soul.

The Face in the Night Sky was born from an intimate conversation with Spirit that continued for three consecutive cycles of the moon. Our language was poetry. I heard the first poem in the quiet of a New Moon morning. The poems that followed were preserved in the order they were received.

I invite you into this timeless conversation.
As you enter a poem's landscape, look for the strand that draws you deeper. Linger for a while to explore how your life intertwines. I hope this experience inspires you to discover a new way of being and a deeper connection with your soul.

NEW MOON 1

blank mind

Emptied of thoughts from the past
spaciousness arises

In the vast realm of the void
knowledge disappears
striving ceases to exist
there is no destination

With nowhere to go and nothing to do
the illusion of separation vanishes

You become one with everything

In the timeless space of the blank mind
beyond the body and the self
the pristine nature of existence is felt

perfection

Nothing out of place
all in perfect order
the ultimate control
of even the smile on your face.

Appearances are foremost
what others think, imperative
scrutinizing self-evaluation

You are of the utmost importance.

Words are highly managed
feelings well restrained
a master of illusion
manipulation's the social game.

Striving for perfection...
What is the result?

A thick fog of separation
void of deep intimacy
your precious self
a stranger

Under the grip of mind's perfection,
the loss of you is inevitable.

containment

Cherish the space
your body inhabits.
Claim it.
It belongs to you.

Be discriminant
as to who you invite in
or share your spirit-home with.

This containment
is your superpower.
Your golden light
at the end of the rainbow.

Your life's creation
arises from this precious sphere
of earth's vibrancy.

Nurture the space
where your soul journey
begins and ends

Cleanse
Purify
Refine

Treasure this lifetime destination
Make it your work of art.

loneliness

In a crowd of people, she feels alone
an unseen girl
looking in the mirror of obscurity.

Too afraid to shine her light,
she shrinks
into a tiny speck of dust.

If she is bright and powerful
others who crave to be big
will find a way to make her small.

Through words or hand
as she dims
they will alight.

Lost in the maze
of unkind words
and hurtful actions

She turns inward
seeking truth.

alone

We enter this world alone.
We leave this world alone.
This earth journey
is meant to be traveled alone.

People will come and go
value their acquaintance
understand the significance
of your meeting.

The company you seek
is of soul and body
a union within yourself.

Find this,
and then one becomes two
and the truth becomes clear
You are never alone.

shadow

An unexpected gift
a delightful treasure
Shadow's sweetness
too great to measure.

The depth of her gaze
is bold and far reaching
her growl and her wail
a profound teaching.

She makes herself big
when a predator is near
her fierce stance of power
makes him cower in fear.

To the top of the tree
she climbs to great heights
like the Spirit of Raven
bound to take flight.

Traveling through time
adrift on soul's tides
she appears in a dream
her bright spirit abides.

Under the face
in the dark night sky
we're deep in thick forest
with stars shining up high.

Around the fire we dance
feet grounded to earth
in sacred ritual
of death and rebirth.

true origin

Unraveling memories
tightly wound together
false perceptions
slowly revealed.

Each singular memory
a movie, paused in time
exposing the intricate details
of your earth body's truth.

The delivery
of mind-body wisdom
at deep heart's door
sparks the essence
of your true origin.

Participation is needed
in this investigation
to track the evidence
of this historic replay.

wisdom seeker

With senses alight,
you are escorted to
the buried feelings
that have pierced your heart.

The Wisdom Seeker
draws you into the darkness
of the sacred well.

Diving into deep waters
you return
to long-forgotten landscapes

environment
surface layer
secondary
primary

In this realm of soul navigation
the ultimate destination
is remembered.

silence

Silence beckons you to its door
inviting you in
to its mysterious home

Residing in the beginning
Residing at the end
It is one
with all of existence.

Silence initiates and follows
    heartbeat
    breath
    thought
    spoken word
    sound

Within the dwelling of Silence
cells listen
while body awaits instruction
The mind is at rest.

Light vibrates with anticipation
Dark dances with color
The Eternal Soul is heard

In the space of Silence
Intelligence is in motion.

one heart wisdom

Through this lifetime
and then another
one momentary recall
invites your presence

This instant replay
lives within you
beyond form
transcending time
backward and forward

Two lives become one.

What you resist
you draw near
What you seek
distances itself

The desire to grasp or repel
to separate or attach is
One Heart Wisdom
offering you a front row seat
to a premiere feature

Accept her invitation
Follow her lead
Cross the threshold

Move beyond the lines of form
to illuminate irrevocable truth.

surface layer

Averting my eyes
from my own self-reflection,
I play the part of a fictional character
in a bestselling novel.

In a replicated costume
of one who is well liked,
my true self is concealed
under a surface layer

Full transparency
is replaced by a painting
of a pretty picture.

I am a brand-new luxury car
with all the extras.
A gourmet meal
served on a silver platter.
I am Happiness all dressed up
in the most convincing disguise.

Beneath the surface layer
basking in the reality of me,
I sink into the life raft of truth.

I don't need mirrors
your acknowledgement
or applause for my leading role
in life's performance

I see my face
with its countless expressions
and the worn lines
of one who lives freely

I see my body
gliding through life
at my direction
as if it's a puppet on a string

As I gaze into the sacred well
of my own reflection,
the distorted view of the false self
becomes crystal clear.

instant replay

Stuck in a loop
going round and round
wherever you exit
The Return will be found.

Each strategy attempted
the new and the old
first tried or resurrected
the same story is told.

You can rewrite the script
one hundred times
create different versions
yet speak the same lines.

In one way or another
even starting again
the same destination
is where you will end.

The route is well traveled
navigation is set
hope is the fuel
the gambler's bet.

This time is different
the situation will change
or you can prevent it
from becoming deranged.

A quick fantasy tale
could be the prescription
to change the narrative
of this repeating infliction.

Or ignore it completely
numb out in resistance
avoid what you're feeling
and deny its existence.

This instant replay
is ingrained in your mind
to exit the loop,
Deep Truth you must find.

Stay present, engaged
see the part you are playing
fully understand
the high price you are paying.

Be aware of the impulse
to change or prevent
to hope once again
your time is well spent.

Observe your actions
change the behavior
to stop the replay
become your own savior.

trying

Before is waiting
for After to arrive.

After is the endgame
with the winning score.

Before is the yellow stoplight
stuck in time,
the waiting room
without a number.

It's the plane ride
circling in fog
unable to land.

Trying is the end result
in backward motion
knocking at the door of Before.

It's an attempt
to convince yourself
that action is in motion.

Your compelling argument
is before the jury.

Do you actually want
what you will find?

When the pitcher that's full
pours only empty excuses,
After never arrives.

Siphon off the surface layer of trying
and fill up your reservoir
with Begin Now.

Then, After will become
your favorite destination.

polarity

What I seek
I will not find
What I resist
will come to me

The tides of polarity
pull me into adversity
with earth's natural way

Harmony is on retreat

Within the perceptions
of the polarized self
The One is forgotten
in the illusion of two

In the dual mirrors
of separation
I draw the line
and never cross it

Harmony is on the other side

With one on top
and one diminished
it might seem
Mind has an advantage
in this illusory game

until Reality
plays its best hand.

road trip

The open road beckons me to distant lands
far removed from the unexplored terrain
of my inner landscape

Gazing through the window of Soul
I see the many shattered pieces
looking for a place to call home

The urge
to leave it all behind
is strong.

Traveling the open road
I am free from the discomfort
of my fragmented self

Yet a road trip
like a mirage in the desert
most likely will not quench Soul's thirst

I count on many fingers
the escapes I have made
under the pretense of a needed vacation.

This time instead of running off
to faraway places
in an attempt to distract myself

I will allow Soul's navigation
to escort me down the untraveled roads
of the inner journey.

calm waters

No more diving off the high board
into life's swimming pool
or being pushed off the rocky cliffs edge
into dark waters.

Nor will I be pulled into
the tumultuous waves of high tide
or struggle as I swim upstream
against the current.

I seek calm waters,
the soothing balm of a warm salt bath
a tranquil swim in a still lake
the effortless flow of river's stream.

I have had my fill of crashing waves
that knock me off my feet
tumbling me in a daze
back to reality's shore.

Instead, I seek to glide across
the glassy surface of time
in a new chartered sailboat
every need attended to
my plate abundantly full.

In calm waters,
I float between the realms
of heaven and earth
seeing my reflection
in the clear pool of the Sacred.

alignment

Within the alliance of opposites
in the realm of the undefined,
the next best thing arrives
in the most unexpected way.

Beyond mind's false perceptions of
good and bad
right and wrong
inadequate and enough
Alignment is in perpetual motion.

Wrong leads you to right
bad results in good
inadequate is precisely enough
better and more arrive at full.

Through the lens of the unmet need,
the dissatisfied seeker
always finds what he's looking for.

Accept the unappreciated gift
to discover what is truly missing.

quiet mind

At first, a worn recording
of familiar phrases
occupies your mind
Thoughts crowd the empty space
demanding to be heard

One thought might move
to the forefront
seeking your undivided attention

Yet if you absorb stillness
long enough
Quiet sneaks in
It's arrival wraps you
in a dark green shawl of ease

Cloaked in earth-rooted nature
your body sinks
into remembering

Soon, Silence
will accompany you
offering Eternity's song

early morning

I welcome the softness
of morning light
where words form poems
and earth's music is heard

Here, Breath sighs deeply
Body relishes in earth's density
Soul fills in the empty spaces

I delight in the luxury
of early morning

Love unfolds here

the gathering

Echoes of past slowly arrive
lost and found have a reunion
welcome them to this gathering
it's your soul's communion.

Get to know how they mingle
and why they come together
notice how you feel
with each message they deliver.

No matter how annoying
don't turn anyone away
be curious to discover
the important part they play.

Pay attention to the timing
of their discreet arrival
especially to the ones
that predict your joy's survival.

in the stillness

In the stillness you will find
Spirit's greatest gift
an open door for truth
to expose your veiled myth

If you listen deeply
and remain open to receive
wisdom will come pouring in
your heart will not deceive

unnamed

People name us
and mold us like clay
sculpting our identities
into whoever they believe
we should be.

I choose to be unnamed.
I am who I know myself to be.

A lineage of names
all strung together
carrying forth
lifetimes of history.

Is this a history
I choose to bring forward?

I am not a brand
labeled for a lifetime
packaged to please the masses.

I won't be shaped by others
or pulled into places
where I don't belong.

Nor will I be coerced into
an altered version
of my originality.

I choose to be unnamed.
I am who I know myself to be.

breath of life

First Breath of Life

In union with air
a steady pace begins
in tune with earth's rhythm
to perpetuate Being

Breath's tempo:
at rest
still
in motion
picking up speed
full capacity

Breath's music:
breathless
shallow
inhale
full

deep
exhale
winded
panting
gasping

In union with body,
an intimate dialogue
of earth's journey
back to its ancient home

Last Breath of Life.

reclaimed

A new creation
carelessly set aside
deemed unworthy

Piece by piece
taken apart
recycled
like scrap metal

mind
body
heart
spirit

Each fragment
of the whole
available for others
who will benefit.

One day,
a wise man
saw her shattered self
and offered to help

Undaunted
by the several
missing pieces
seeking retrieval

he taught her how to search
for what was missing
and follow the sacred path
back to wholeness

Piece by piece,
she reclaimed
all that was lost
and forgotten.

present

Your relationship with Past is behind you
Make friends with Present

Enjoy this new friend's company
and be ready for the gift you will receive

Savor the moment

Don't gossip about Past
or anticipate Future's arrival,
give Present your undivided attention

Hope you don't say goodbye too soon
and rush off to meet the stranger
named Future

It's better to let Future surprise you
when you are completely satisfied
with Present's company

When Present converges with Future,
meaning is found

luxury

Indulge
in the luxury
of stillness

in the soft essence of silence
the spaciousness of a quiet mind

Indulge
in the luxury
of time

in the expansive aura of nothing planned
the timelessness of freedom

Indulge
in the luxury
of space

in the calm nature of simplicity
the elegance of emptiness

the river

Life on earth is a dream
that carries us forward
first breath to last breath
aligned with the waters of Spirit

Desire sets our placement
on earth's wide channel,
while the river itself
never changes course

We can navigate life's waters
in gentle fashion
accepting the undercurrent
that draws us deeper

Or we can veer widely off course
to face earth's boulders
and rising rapids

Either way,
whether we force a direction
grip tightly or surrender

the river already knows
its destination

Eventually, we realize that
we can arrive at our final breath
either through struggle or ease

the journey

I traverse the vast desert floor
bare feet on dusty ground
yearning to nourish my body
and quench my soul's thirst

The journey begins

Eternally humbled
I enter earth's boundless ocean
diving into its cleansing waters
longing for saturation

The journey deepens

Cold and breathless
I climb the northern summit
careening steep rocky cliffs
searching for a higher view

The journey becomes clear

As I wander in the tranquil forest
caressed by the soft light of solitude
I join the deep-rooted pines
reaching for heaven

The journey greets its return
I rest

NEW MOON 2

the unsought

If you seek something
before you are ready
it will float on the surface
unable to penetrate.

Two will never become one.

If you seek something
that doesn't belong to you
the divide will be too great
for it to be felt.

Two will always remain two.

Yet if something unsought
finds its way to you
no time or space
will keep you apart.

The One was always The One.

your life movie

It's easy to get lost
to have the veil of the dead
placed over you.

The words others recite in your ear
become your only memory.
The images of what they see
are now your movie screen.

Before you know it,
you are in the audience
watching yourself play the part
of a false rendition of you.

Walk out of the theatre.

Discard the old projections
and dismiss those who want
to do the final editing.

Stop seeking the reviews
hoping that you have
pleased the critics.

Write a new script.

Allow your soul
to be the director
of your life movie.

the cage

A barrier
between you and life
just beyond reach

Meant to protect
it separates
me from you

Isolated
like a caged bird
unable to fly

One thought
one belief
one experience
or simply delusion
can become the cage
that splits your life in two

Turned inward,
it's the dividing line
between you
and your heart

A beautiful life
before your eyes
kept at a distance

An experience
that arrives
floating on air
untouchable

The cage
is the void
between you
and Wholeness

Open the door
Fly free
Let life's breath fill you

self-doubt

I often stumble
on the ridgeline of self-doubt
interrupting my smooth stride with Yes.

It trips me up, I fall
into a chasm of complicated tunnels
often leading to dead ends.

Self-doubt is the wide gap
between earth identity
and soul knowing.

Yet in the space
where self-doubt echoes
silence resides as well.

In the depths of silence
you can shine a light
on the darkness of doubt.

Expose it
then send it off
in another direction.

But before you do, understand
how it found a home in you
and why it's so well fed.

The knowing of self
the understanding of doubt
is the clear pathway back
to the higher ground of Yes.

the stranger

In intricate detail
events of past and present
interweave throughout lifetimes

Each experience transports you
through time, backward and forward
the nonlinear way

Sudden arrivals
come with understanding
and sometimes confusion and pain

A revealed destiny
illuminates the path
a journey only you can foretell

You seek what is known
find comfort in what's real
but the truth is you are a stranger

Your journey is vast,
this lifetime
a speck of dust

The knowing of who you are
is a faraway view of a mountaintop
seen from a fogged window

With this in mind,
find delight in the unnamed
versions of you

Greet them like a new lover
enthralled with every nuance

Embrace the stranger
Dance with the mystery of you

listen deeply

Hear the voice
that directs you
to listen deeply.

Hear the voice
inside you
who questions.

Who is evaluating
the crowd
in this gathering space
called Mind?

Listen to those
you have invited
to this exclusive
inner sanctum.

They reside
in the center of all things
pulled inward
aligned with the One.

Listen deeply
with your whole body
in union with Soul.

Listening
is the greatest gift
you can offer
the unheard.

voices of past

Past thoughts crowd the room
of this gathering.

Listen to what they have to say
and get to know the ones
who are the most popular.

Discover when they took
their first breath.
They are the storytellers lost in time.

Behind the bold voices of past,
present thoughts wait patiently.

Seek out their company.
They are the observers
conversing with Now.

When you discover why the past
has shown up to this
present moment gathering,

Wisdom is found.

burning desire

What do you believe
you should want?

What do you
think you want?

What do you
truly want?

You are twirling around
the great circle of Desire's fire
dancing with Confusion.

The amber coals
of seeking and yearning
keep the fire burning brightly,
while desire's sparking embers
whirl in the air
but quickly burn out.

You must add new fuel
to feed the fire
more and more and more.

Yet when you see through
the smoke of illusion
this internal fire brings
you will pour the translucent water
of Spirit Wisdom
to extinguish it.

And when you see a fire rise
from bare, cold ground
with no external means of ignition

You will know this flame
burning brightly
is born from Soul.

expectation

It's hard to accept people as they are
without naming
what you hope they'll change.

At first greeting, or shortly thereafter
you have already determined
what it is you think they need.

A customized script you hand to them
if their part is played well
approval is granted.

But if no change occurs
the cords that bind you
only pull tighter.

You can throw them a rope
and pull them up to the next plateau
as you climb the mountain peak.

Or you can free yourself
from expectation
accept exactly what you see

Find the Soul
within the journey
and converse with Destiny.

Or better yet,
choose to climb the mountain
accompanied by The Stranger.

memories

We all face difficulties in life.

People hurt us
with their words,
and sometimes
with their hands.

These memories
become embedded
in our mind and body.
We can't escape them.

Stuck on replay,
we hear the same story
we play the same part
we recreate the same experience.

We are unable to see
our damaged self-identity.

Yet with awareness,
we can understand
the difficult path we walk.

We can feel
the pain inside us
and accept how it was born.

We can untangle
the words that hurt us
and discard their hidden thorns.

With each step we take forward
we can experience something new.

People who inspire us
with their words.

People who nurture us
with their hands.

These memories
become embedded
in our mind and body.
We cherish them.

We tell a new story
We play a new part
We create a new experience.

the new world

Between the new
and the old world
the void is vast

I can no longer
leap across
to the other side

The scent of the old world
drifts on the wind
farther and farther away

The voices I hear
are faint echoes
of a distant past

Pictures fade quickly

I yearn to touch the familiar
yet there is no part of me
left behind

I have arrived in the New World

the path ahead

Where I began
now seen from a distance
Looking back, at the many exhales
where Breath has been

Stories are etched
on ancient walls of mind
while past visions
no longer linger in the wind

The river of tears is dried up

Before the light of dawn
the path ahead can't be seen
Mystery swirls in the air
waiting to be absorbed by matter

I inhale deeply

the discovery

Trembling
at the center of being
in a whirlwind of thought
a precious artifact is unearthed

I sift through the settled dust
seeking to unbury
the deepest truth

I face the promise
of a great discovery
as each treasured piece
wants to be found

Brought into vision
held near to heart
a new story is told

be brave

Listen to your soul
recite its poetry

Quiet the inner voices
that send you down
the known path

Be brave.

Arrive in a foreign land
Speak a new language
Walk on untraveled roads

Let the sun soothe your soul
the stars light your way
guide you through your fear

Let the heart nourishment of earth
quell the ground under your feet
walk steadily ahead

Be brave.

soul wisdom

Some memories are
imprinted on your body,
never to be erased.

Lying on the surface
they may fade overtime
but not vanish completely.

You can attempt to erase them
or you can let these memories
fully absorb into your being.

See them
Listen to them
Touch them
Feel them

Become one with them

This eternal embrace
offers deeper understanding
a new interpretation
Soul Wisdom.

travel deep

No pending breath
Nothing lying on the surface
unabsorbed

No trick of the mind
keeping my soul
at a distance

Past and present
are intimate lovers
speaking only truth

Every part of me is
seen
heard
felt
understood
valued

My breath travels deep

the promise

A fire spreads far and wide
burning all in sight
across the land.

The planted seed of Soul
already knows
what will break through
the scorched surface.

It has been lying dormant
cultivated ages ago
watered and fed
slowly grown.

In preparation for its arrival
a drenching rain
soaks the fertile ground
of the long-awaited promise.

Silence marks the entry
of this timeless return.

soul impression

When your soul resides
in its earthly home,
what it sees out the window
is inner-reality.

Body's security system
wants to monitor all
but Consciousness is rarely seen
never mind detected.

So, all you can do
is respond in the moment,
allowing your soul
to guide your actions.

This soul impression
in one single moment
has the power to alter
eternity's creation.

full moon's light

Some need to see beauty
to have a rise,
I want to feel beauty
deep inside

Some need to touch gold
to feel rich,
I want to feel wealth
traveling through my veins
and out my breath

I pass on the self-induced,
sought-out high
that fills you up
then leaves you empty inside

Instead, I walk
in full moon's light
following the path
my soul ignites

spirit wind

Toss into the wind all mind's ideas
of the direction your life should head
as Spirit Wind has a mind of its own,
The Return is drifting in

It blows into your life quite unexpected,
a whirlwind of the unnamed
Mind wants to grasp what's floating on air,
but surrender is all it obtains

When the wind quiets and the dust settles,
Truth is what you will find
Pick it up with your hands
hold it close to your heart,
in reverence of the Divine

lift it up

It's been delivered, The Gift
left on your doorstep.
Lift it up
and hold it in your hands.

You might wonder
where it came from
and why it was delivered
to you now.

What is hidden beneath
its earthly exterior?

With mind and body engaged
participate in its opening.
Reveal all it contains.

Lift it up
from its earthly origin
into the realm of Soul.

the sacred well

You sit at the bottom of the sacred well
within its deep emptiness
there is no return to your old ways

The dark is absorbed in your bones
breath stills, while you await
earth's cleansing waters to revive you

As the sacred well slowly fills
once again, Soul lifts you higher

With clear vision you rise
to greet the light of a new world

meet me

Meet me where angels fly
and eternal bells ring
above the opposition
in every human being

Meet me where truth travels
from ground to soul's sky
beyond the confusion
of many past lives

Meet me where eagle's wings
spread far and wide
free from human sorrow
and the great divide

Meet me where old souls unite
where Divine showers
shed new light

NEW MOON 3

the 11 expressway

Beyond words or explanation
Truth speaks
It's a felt sense
a clear path to Yes or No

No mental roadblocks
delays or dead ends
No emotional hills
or switchbacks

Just straight open highway

The 11 Expressway
leading to energetic alignment
Free-flowing movement
heading in the right direction

Alignment in its purest form

inhale deeply

It has come to you,
waking a memory
of a time long forgotten
a life carried on the wind.

Let it blow away
the cobwebs and the dust.
Let it clear what lies on the surface
and unsettle the stagnant deep within.

Invite its fierce nature
to swirl around inside you.
Where does it surge
and then finally land?

Inhale deeply
Feel its power
as it transforms
your next breath.

interwoven

No line drawn in the sand
property line to protect
or boundary to cross

No ticking clock
calendar to verify
or moon cycle to track

No before or after
then, now or soon
start or stop

Only continuum,
time and space
interwoven

Fluid motion expanding
in every direction
no end in sight

Nothing to begin
or complete
only to Be

Use each moment
to participate
in this evolution

Every thought, every act
becomes the whole
You are one
You are all

Like the organisms in nature
too many to count
perpetuating Earth

Like the cells in your body
billions of Beings
resulting in You

What are you creating?

going to

I am going to do
something important
but not now
most likely later
often tomorrow.

I talk about a future plan
a desire for action
the hope for change.

But what I am going to do
and what I actually do
are two different things
kept apart by words
hanging on the air
of uncertainty.

It's much better to be silent
move into action
and then speak about
what has been done.

I will let my words
swirl around inside me
until momentum is found.

the gap

It's not an indicator
of who you are

The gap is the space
that resides between you
and another

The space where you
effortlessly meet
or tragically fall apart.

You can't narrow the distance
or fill in the gap
no matter how hard you try

Not even perfect words
and determined action
will help you cross the line

Only energetic alignment
gives rise to being together
with The One.

love match

One spark ignites
a deep remembrance
setting two hearts aflame

Kindling a love match
one that is slowly fed
and then well-tended

A smoldering fire
soon left
to dwindle into ash
extinguished

Until we meet again

separate

Walls and windows of the mind
a world kept separate
by an imaginary line.

Across the border
lives intertwine
and then unravel before your eyes.

Within time and space
there is no wall
that separates The One from all.

When brought together
through earth and heaven
you part the ways where the veil is thin.

You merge the gap
expose the illusion
and free yourself from heart's confusion.

.

earth serenity

Awaken from your deep sleep
with eyes that see
and a body that senses
Earth's serenity.

Air in its leisure
comes to you.
Water's effortless flow
lands at your feet.

Primordial elements
sustain your breath,
while nature's beauty
surrounds and fills.

The ebb and flow
of earth's body
supports you,
safely within its edges.

daily dance

My soul is here
ready for her daily dance
with this body of mine

Feet grounded to earth,
I embrace her
as we move through the day
in fluid motion

Mind receptive, heart full
in rhythm with nature's pulse,
I am whole

Spirit joins us in this lifetime love

immersed

No one can pull me in to their turmoil
I am contained

This sphere of self
surrounds and protects my body

I can choose
how I want to share myself
when I want to share myself
if I want to share myself

I stand strong in my own being
immersed in the energy of me

Light
Wisdom
Truth
Strength

I live with
My soul
My body
Spirit

unknown waters

Waking up and starting over,
what lies ahead for me?

I am treading unknown waters,
only unfamiliar land I see.

No path ahead or options to choose
my soul companion is a blank mind.

Until I see a message written from the sky
or hear my guide's instruction

I will breathe deeply
and enjoy the silence.

ABOUT THE AUTHOR

I revel in my walk with soul, my body grounded to earth, with my sight on the moon. When I am not in dialogue with Spirit, writing, or guiding others you will find me in nature walking and listening. – Lana Lensman

www.ingramcontent.com/pod-product-compliance
Lightning Source LLC
Chambersburg PA
CBHW050857150626
46549CB00013B/2673